How do I use this scheme?

Key Words with Peter and Jane has three parallel series, each containing twelve books. All three series are written using the same carefully controlled vocabulary. Readers will get the most out of **Key Words** with Peter and Jane when they follow the books in the pattern 1a, 1b, 1c; 2a, 2b, 2c and so on.

• Series a
gradually introduces and repeats new words.

• Series b
provides further practice of these same words, but in a different context and with different illustrations.

• Series c
uses familiar words to teach **phonics** in a methodical way, enabling children to read increasingly difficult words. It also provides a link to writing.

LADYBIRD BOOKS

UK | USA | Canada | Ireland | Australia
India | New Zealand | South Africa

Ladybird Books is part of the Penguin Random House group of companies
whose addresses can be found at global.penguinrandomhouse.com.

www.penguin.co.uk   www.puffin.co.uk   www.ladybird.co.uk

First published 1964
This edition 2009, 2014, 2016
Copyright © Ladybird Books Ltd, 1964
001

A CIP catalogue record for this book is
available from the British Library

ISBN: 978-1-409-30115-8

Printed in China

Key Words

with Peter and Jane

6a — Our friends

written by W. Murray
illustrated by M. Aitchison

Here is a girl who lives on a farm. She is Pam, and she lives on this big farm with her mother and father. Pam likes to live here.

She wants to help her father with the farm work this afternoon. She takes the two big horses to water. Pam is on one of them. Her dog is with her.

Pam can do other work. She can look after the pigs or help to milk the cows. She likes to work on the farm after school.

Peter and Jane go to school with Pam. Pam sits with Jane in school. Pam likes Jane, and Jane likes Pam. Jane and Peter are soon going to the farm for tea. Then, one afternoon, Pam will go to Jane's house for tea.

new words
4   Pam   lives   mother   father

Here are the children at tea in the farm-house. Jane is going to have some milk, and Pam gives Peter some cakes. She talks to the brother and sister about the farm.

"I will take you to see the horses after tea," she says. "I know you like them best."

"Yes," says Peter, "I like the horses best on your farm, and then I like the pigs."

"I like your cows best," says Jane. "I want to see the man milk them."

"Have a good tea," says Pam. "Eat some more cake."

As they eat they can see out of the window. They look at the sun on the hill. "You must like to live here on your farm," says Jane.

"Yes, I like to live here," says Pam.

---

new words   **best**   **your**

The three children go to see the horses. All three of them like horses. "Here they are," says Pam. "This is where they live."

"The big one is best," says Peter. "Let me get up on him." The others help Peter up. "Thank you," he says, "I like it up here."

Jane has some apples in a bag. She takes out three of them. "Can we give them apples?" she asks.

"Yes," says Pam, "apples are good for them."

Pam talks about the horses. "They like me," she says. "I make them work, but they like their work."

"Your horses like their apples," says Jane. "Look, they want some more."

The horses eat more apples. The three children pat the horses and talk to them.

Pam says, "Now we will look at the pigs."

new words

three   their

"This is where the pigs live," says Pam. "There are some baby ones."

Pam's father is with the pigs. He is going to give them something to eat. "Pigs like to eat," says Pam's father.

"Look at the baby pigs," says Jane. "I like the baby ones."

"Yes," says Peter, "they are so little and the others so big."

new word   baby

"See how your baby pigs like their mother," says Jane to Pam.

"Yes," says Pam, "they know who looks after them."

"The cows are going by," says Pam's father to the three children. "I help to milk them. I have to go now."

"Can we see some more of the farm?" asks Peter.

"Yes," says Pam, "come on then, let us go for a walk." The three children walk round the farm where Pam lives.

"We like going round your farm like this," says Peter to Pam.

They come to the water. Peter wants to look at the fish. He gives them something to eat.

"I can see some big fish and their baby ones," he says. "They are going round and round."

Pam and Jane get some flowers. Jane looks up. "I can see your father by the farm-house," she says, "and there are the men at work."

"What is the time?" asks Peter. "It must soon be time to go home."

"I can see a car going to the farm-house," says Jane. "It is our Dad's car. He and Mum have come for us. It is time to go."

new words   round   time

13

Peter's and Jane's mother and father have come for their children. They have come in their car. Pam's father talks to Jane's father, and her mother comes out of the house with some eggs.

"What big eggs!" says Jane. "They must be the best."

"The eggs are for you," says Pam's mother to Jane's mother.

"Thank you," says Jane's mother. "It is good of you. We all like eggs."

The three children talk. "Thank you for a good time," says Peter. "We liked going round your farm."

"The baby pigs are sweet," says Jane.

"Come and see them again soon," says Pam.

"You must come to our house," says Jane's mother to Pam. "We are going away soon to the sea, but you must come to see us after that."

"Yes, please," says Pam.

---

new word

eggs

The children are away at the sea. As they eat their eggs they look out of the window. They can see the sea and the boats. Their friend Tom is by the boats. He lives by the sea all the time.

"Our friend Tom knows all about boats," says Peter. "He is the best one to take us out in a boat this afternoon."

In comes their mother. "Eat up your eggs," she says, "and then I want you to come round the shops with me."

"Can we go out with our friend Tom this afternoon?" asks Peter.

"Yes," says Mother, "you can see your friend Tom. He will look after you. Here is your father," she says, "so come on, you two."

---

new words   friend   Tom

The three in the boat are Jane, Peter, and their friend Tom. Jane has her doll, Ann, with her. She says that Ann likes boats.

They are out at sea in their boat. The children like it on the water. They can see other boats and the houses. There is no danger.

Tom stops the boat for a time, so that Peter can fish. Then he talks to the two children. Tom knows how to fish as he lives by the sea. He helps Peter and Jane to get some big fish.

Jane lets her doll Ann see the fish.

"We will give them to our mother and father," says Peter.

"Then we will have fish for tea," says Jane. "We all like fish. Do you want some, Tom?"

---

new words

doll Ann

The sun is out today. Jane and Peter are in the sun by the sea when they see their friend Tom. Jane has Ann, her doll, with her again.

Tom sits on a boat and talks about the sea, about boats, and about fish. He likes to live by the sea, and he likes to talk about the sea. He likes it best of all when he is in a boat, on the sea, in the sun.

Their friend Tom helps boys or girls when they want to go out in a boat, or to fish. He says there are times when he has to jump into the water to help boys or girls who are in danger.

new words

today   when

Peter and Jane have come home today with their mother and father.

"It is good to be home," says Mother, as the car stops. She tells Peter to help Father with the bags. "Help Dad get the things from the car," she says.

Then Mother tells Jane to go next door for the cat. "Be a good girl," she says, "and go to our friends next door for the cat."

Jane puts down her doll, Ann, and off she runs.

Father and Peter take the bags from the car into the house and come out again. "Now we have time to get the dog," says Father.

As they go off, Jane comes from next door with her cat.

new words
tells   next   door

Mr and Mrs Green live next door to Jane and Peter. Mr and Mrs Green are friends of Jane's mother and father.

Today, Peter's father tells Mr Green about the good time they have had by the sea. Mr Green is by his car. He is going to the shops with Mrs Green.

Mrs Green talks to Jane's mother, who asks her to get some eggs for her at the shops.

"I like to see your two children play with my three," says Mrs Green. "Look at them now, they do have fun." The two mothers see their children play.

Pat likes to be with the boys. He runs round them with a ball, as they play their game.

The two girls like it best when they can look after the baby.

---

new words

Mr Mrs Green

This is Bob. He is the boy who lives next door to Peter and Jane. His mother and father are Mr and Mrs Green.

Bob is Peter's best friend. Every day Bob comes round to see Peter. Every day Bob helps Peter do his work, and then Peter helps Bob with his. Then, every day, they play games at home or go out.

Today, when Bob asks Peter to come out to play, Peter tells him his father said he must work for some time.

"I will help you," says Bob. "I like to help."

The two boys soon do the work and then go off for the afternoon.

"Let us take your dog," says Bob. "He likes to come with us."

"Yes," says Peter, "come on, Pat."

new words

Bob   every   day

26

Here is Peter with his best friend Bob who lives next door. Every day Peter and Bob go out to play.

"What do you want to do today?" asks Peter.

Bob says, "Let us go for a walk to see what we can find."

The two boys walk by the trees down by the water. They look into the water to find some fish. Pat wants to jump into the water, but Peter keeps him out.

The two boys look at the birds in the trees. They like to see them. Then Bob

finds some birds' eggs. He tells Peter about them. The two boys look at the eggs but they do not take them.

new words
find   birds

Here are Peter and Bob again. Today they have come to see if they can find some rabbits. They do find some. The rabbits cannot see the boys if they keep by the trees. There are birds in the trees.

"The rabbits come here every day," Bob tells Peter. "If they see us they will go," he says.

"The baby ones run round and round," says Peter, "and the big ones keep a look out all the time."

"There are one, two, three, four rabbits," says Peter.

"Yes, there are four," says Bob. "I can see four."

Then the big rabbit sees the boys. He tells the others, and off they all go.

"There they go," says Peter.

"Yes," says Bob, "off they all go. They saw danger."

new words

if   four

The girl with Jane is Mary. She is Bob's sister. Mary lives next door to Jane, and her mother and father are Mr and Mrs Green. Mary and Jane are very good friends.

Mary likes to play with Jane very much, and she comes into Jane's house every day. Jane can go next door into Mary's house if she wants to.

Mr and Mrs Green like Jane very much, and they let her come into their house when she likes.

Jane and Mary play with Jane's doll Ann. Mary likes Jane's doll, so Jane lets her play with it when she wants to.

Today Jane tells Mary about her friend Tom who lives by the sea. She tells Mary about the day she was in the boat.

new words

Mary   very   much

Mary and Jane are going to give their dolls some tea today. Mary has her own doll, and Jane has her own doll, Ann. The dog is there.

They have some cakes which Mrs Green gave them, and some milk which Jane's mother let them have. Bob gave his sister a bag of sweets, and Jane's brother gave some apples.

new words
own gave

34

Jane gives out the cakes. "One, two, three, four," she says. "There are four of us and the dog." She gets off her chair to give Pat some milk. He likes it very much, and looks as if he wants some more.

Mary gives out the sweets, and then she sees the birds. "We must find something for the birds," she says.

Today Jane finds Mary by her garden. Mary has her own little garden. Her father gave it to her. Every day Mary likes to go to her own garden to look at the flowers.

Mary likes birds, but if she finds them on her garden she makes them fly away. "Fly away," she says to the birds. "I don't want you on my garden."

Bob has his own little garden, and so have Peter and Jane. All four children like their gardens very much.

Pat is with Jane, and she says to him, "Don't go on there, Pat. Don't go on the garden." Pat runs after the birds as they fly away.

The two girls want to get some flowers for their mothers.

new words		
garden	fly	don't

The little girl in the garden is Molly. She is Mary's sister and she is three. She has her own toy bird and she can make it fly. Molly is going round and round to make her bird fly. Her father gave her this toy.

Mary is coming with Pat, and the dog wants to run after Molly's toy bird.

"Don't, Pat," says Mary, "don't run." She pulls at the dog. Pat likes little Molly very much. He wants to play with her. Molly loves the dog.

The little girl loves all four children and they all love her.

Mary looks after Molly if Mrs Green is not there. She has Molly's hat. She puts the hat on her sister. "Keep your hat on, Molly," she says.

new words

Molly   loves   hat

It is hot today. Molly likes to play with water on a hot day. Here she is in the garden with her toys and the dog.

The dog is hot, so Molly gives him some water. Then she puts some water on the dog. Pat likes it as he is hot. He is very wet now. Molly is wet, and the toys are wet.

Here comes Bob. "Put some water on the flowers," he says to Molly. "It is good for them. The sun makes them so hot." He helps Molly water the flowers in their own gardens.

Then he plays with Molly and the dog. They all love to play in the sun. Bob says, "Molly, don't take off your hat or get it wet."

new words
hot   wet

It is a hot day again. It was wet, but now the sun is out. Peter and Jane are on the top of a big red bus. They are going down the street to the station.

They are going to see their grandmother and grandfather. Father is at work today, so he is not with the children. Mother is with them.

The two children love their grandmother and grandfather. Jane likes her
grandmother to take her round her big
garden, and Peter wants his grandfather
to help him to make a boat. Grandfather
is good at this.

Pat is on the bus with them. He is a
good dog on the bus and in the train.

new words
grandmother   grandfather

Grandmother and Grandfather live in an old house. They are at home all the time. Grandfather is old and he does not go out to work. He likes to work in the garden and sit by the fire and read.

Grandmother is old, like Grandfather. She does not do very much work. She likes to walk in her garden.

They have a big garden with trees and flowers. Grandmother and Grandfather sit in the garden. They look at the birds as they fly about.

There is a big dog in this house, and he likes Pat. They are old friends.

Here are Mother and the children at the house. Grandmother comes out. "It is good to see you," she says. "Come in. Let us all have some tea."

"Dad wants us to give you his love," says Jane.

---

new words

old does

Here are the children at their school. They all like going to their school, because they like the teacher. The teacher is an old friend of theirs. She loves children.

The teacher says, "Let us talk about the police." She draws a policeman. "The policeman is our friend," she says. "I will tell you about the work he does." She talks for some time.

Soon it is time to go home. "The time does fly," says Jane.

Some days Peter and Jane walk home. Today they are going by bus because it is wet. "We don't want to get wet," says Peter.

"We will see Grandmother and Grandfather today," says Jane. "They are coming for tea."

"Good," says Peter, "Grandfather will have my boat with him. I want it very much."

our friends

new words
because   teacher

Pam has come to Jane's home today. Mary and Molly from next door are there. Pam has been to tea before with Jane, and so have Mary and Molly.

Pam says, "Mum wants to ask our teacher to tea because Mum wants to see her. Will you all come?"

"Yes, it will be fun," says Mary. "Molly and I have not been to the farm before."

"I want to come," says Jane. "I have been to the farm before and I like it very much."

The four girls sit down to eat.

Jane says, "The two boys had their tea before us, because they want to play with their boat. Our grandfather gave a boat to Peter, and the boys have been down at the water all day."

new words

been   before

49

Peter and Jane talk before they go to bed. They play with the cat. The dog looks on.

Peter says, "I read at school today that a horse is a man's best friend. I like horses, but my best friend is Bob Green."

"My best friends are Mary and Molly and Pam," says Jane. "I like cats and dogs, and I like the horses we saw at the farm."

"Our teacher is a good friend because she helps us," says Peter.

"Yes," says Jane, "and so does old Tom down by the sea. He has been a good friend to us."

The brother and sister talk about their other friends.

"All our friends help us, and we help them," says Peter. "It is good to help our friends."

no new words

New words used in this book

Total number of new words: 52
Average repetition per word: 13